A TRUE BOOK™

WITHDRAWN

Big Battles of World War II

PETER BENOIT

Children's Press®
An Imprint of Scholastic Inc.
New York Toronto London Auckland Sydney
Mexico City New Delhi Hong Kong
Danbury, Connecticut

Content Consultant
James Marten, PhD
Professor and Chair, History Department
Marquette University, Milwaukee, Wisconsin

Library of Congress Cataloging-in-Publication Data
Benoit, Peter, 1955–
Big Battles of World War II / by Peter Benoit.
   pages cm. — (A true book)
Includes bibliographical references and index.
ISBN 978-0-531-20494-8 (library binding) — ISBN 978-0-531-21729-0 (paperback)
1. World War, 1939–1945—Campaigns—Juvenile literature. 2. Battles—Juvenile literature. I. Title.
D743.7.B46 2014
940.54'2—dc23   2014003933

All rights reserved. Published in 2015 by Children's Press, an imprint of Scholastic Inc.
Printed in The United State of America 113
SCHOLASTIC, CHILDREN'S PRESS, A TRUE BOOK™, and associated logos are trademarks and/or registered trademarks of Scholastic Inc.

1 2 3 4 5 6 7 8 9 10 R 24 23 22 21 20 19 18 17 16 15

Front cover: U.S. marines exploding a cave on Iwo Jima
Back cover: Troops raising the U.S. flag on Iwo Jima

Find the Truth!

Everything you are about to read is true *except* for one of the sentences on this page.

Which one is **TRUE**?

T or F   Germany lost more troops during the Battle of the Bulge than any other nation.

T or F   All U.S. warships survived the attack at Pearl Harbor without damage.

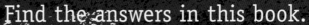

Find the answers in this book.

Contents

THE **BIG** TRUTH!

A New Kind of War

The first kamikaze attack
occurred in 1944.

A soldier reads a newspaper announcing an end to the war in Europe.

Hiroshima, Japan, after being bombed

The Battle of Verdun was the longest and one of the most destructive battles of World War I.

CHAPTER 1

The Beginnings of War

Between 1914 and 1918, Europe experienced a violent conflict. At the time, it was known as the Great War. In those four years, Europe changed. Countries lost or gained land. Some nations came under new governments. However, even when the war ended, people faced many challenges. The fighting had been costly and destructive. Millions of people had died. After the war, jobs and money were hard to come by in many places.

 Today, the Great War is more commonly known as World War I.

Treaty of Versailles

Many countries that had participated in the Great War signed the Treaty of Versailles in 1919. This peace agreement officially blamed Germany for the war. Parts of that country's territory were taken away, and Germany was told to pay other countries for the people and property lost during the war. But the war had seriously weakened Germany's economy. The country struggled to make these payments.

The four main planners of the Treaty of Versailles were, from left to right, British prime minister David Lloyd George, Italian prime minister Vittorio Orlando, French statesman Georges Clemenceau, and American president Woodrow Wilson.

The United States never officially accepted the Versailles Treaty.

Adolf Hitler (front) named himself Führer, or absolute leader, of Germany.

The Rise of the Nazi Party

Some Germans were angry about the treaty and about Germany's weak economy. Many found a solution in the rising Nazi Party and its leader, Adolf Hitler. Hitler spoke of the greatness of the German people above all others. He was elected chancellor of Germany in 1933 and quickly established himself as **dictator**. He built up Germany's army and its air force, called the Luftwaffe. Hitler planned to **expand** the country's borders and establish a powerful German empire, which he called the Third Reich.

Japan rapidly became more industrialized during the 20th century.

Unrest in the Pacific

Germany was not alone in its push for expansion. Japan also started working to gain territory. Part of Japan's reason for this was to obtain **resources**. Japan is an island with a limited supply of oil, metals, and other materials. These resources were increasingly being used to make products in the 20th century. By expanding into other areas, more of these materials would be under Japan's control.

Japan invaded northern China in the early 1930s. As one of the largest countries in the world, China had vast lands and resources. By 1938, Japan had taken over areas across northern and southern China. In the late 1930s, Japan began looking to expand into Southeast Asia and islands in the Pacific Ocean. France, Britain, the United States, and other countries controlled many of these territories.

Japanese soldiers move carefully through rubble in Shanghai, China, in 1932.

Soviet foreign minister Vyacheslav Mikaylovich Molotov (seated) signs the German-Soviet Pact.

Hitler disapproved of smoking. He had photos of the pact signing adjusted to remove any cigarettes.

The War on the Eastern Front

In Europe, Germany first expanded east. In 1939, Germany signed an agreement with the Soviet Union, a country that included what is now Russia and surrounding areas. The agreement stated that Germany and the Soviet Union would not attack each other. Other countries knew about this agreement. But there was also a secret part to it. That part called for splitting the country of Poland, which had borders with Germany and the Soviet Union. Germany wanted western Poland. The Soviets claimed Poland's eastern part.

Invasion of Poland

The German military invaded western Poland on September 1, 1939. The Luftwaffe bombarded troops and towns. This disrupted communications and cleared the way for Germany's tanks and **infantry**. In Poland's defense, Britain and France declared war on Germany two days later. But Germany did not slow down. German tanks reached the Polish capital of Warsaw on September 8. Soon after, Soviet troops flooded across Poland's eastern border.

German troops ride into a Polish village in 1939.

Farmers and their families leave their village in the Soviet Union after it comes under attack.

Moving In

The Nazis hated the Soviet system of government, called Communism. Hitler wanted to take over the country and destroy its government. In June 1941, Germany broke its agreement with the Soviet Union and invaded that country. The Soviets retreated but did not give up. Soldiers and **civilians** burned crops, destroyed bridges and railroad cars, and **evacuated** or moved entire factories. This made it difficult for the Germans to find food, move people and equipment, and gain important factories and weapons.

German soldiers attack a Soviet tank during the Battle of Stalingrad.

Hitler refused to allow the German army to retreat while invading the Soviet Union.

Fighting continued into October and November. Winter approached, and temperatures fell to some of the coldest in the area in decades. The German soldiers were not prepared for the cold, but the Soviets were. The Soviet army finally stopped the Germans outside the capital city of Moscow in the winter of 1941–1942. Months later, the armies fought over Stalingrad. Despite suffering many more **casualties** than the Germans, the Soviet army drove the Germans back.

The Siege of Leningrad

The German army had a stronger hold over Leningrad. Much of the city had been evacuated at the beginning of the invasion, but millions of people remained. They came under **siege** in September 1941. The German army cut Leningrad off from highways and railroads. The city's supplies quickly ran short. By December, Leningrad residents were starving. The siege continued for 872 days, until more Soviet soldiers came and forced the Germans to retreat in 1944.

Drinkable water, like everything else, was difficult to find in Leningrad. Here, residents collect water flowing out of a damaged water pipe.

An Australian tank hides behind an explosion at Tobruk, Libya.

Britain, Australia, Poland, Germany, and Italy all fought at Tobruk during World War II.

CHAPTER 3

The War in North Africa

The war also spread into North Africa. Some of the most continuous fighting took place in Tobruk, Libya. Italy had controlled this important port city since the 1910s. In January 1941, British forces captured Tobruk. In April, Italy worked with Germany to surround the city. Germany, Italy, and Japan together were called the Axis powers. They bombed the city for 240 days. In June 1942, the Axis powers finally captured Tobruk. In November, they lost it again to Britain and its allies, called the Allied forces.

The Battles of El Alamein

While they controlled Tobruk, the Axis troops moved east into Egypt. In July 1942, Allied forces stopped them at El Alamein, a railway station on Egypt's northern coast. El Alamein provided access to the Suez Canal, the shortest route between Europe and the Indian and Pacific Oceans. A second battle began when the Allies struck in October. They had twice the troops and tanks that the Axis military had. After 20 days of fighting, the Axis powers retreated.

British soldiers move through the smoke toward German troops at El Alamein, Egypt.

After El Alamein

The fighting that occurred at El Alamein is still causing casualties. To help defend their positions during World War II, forces planted millions of land mines. Not all of these mines exploded during the war. In fact, experts estimate that as many as 16 million unexploded land mines and shells were left around El Alamein. The buried mines are still dangerous. Since the end of the war, they have caused thousands of casualties among people living in the area.

A New Kind of War

In World War I, airplanes were still a new technology. At first, planes were mostly used to fly over an area to see what the enemy was up to. Before long, designers attached guns and found ways to drop bombs from planes. By World War II, militaries had developed new **tactics** using planes. Two of the most successful examples were the German blitzkrieg and the Japanese kamikaze.

Blitzkrieg means "lightning war" in German. The tactic had two parts. First, the Luftwaffe flew in and attacked enemy communications systems. This left enemy forces confused and disorganized. Next, German tanks entered the battle on land, backed up by infantry. The Luftwaffe provided extra support.

Kamikaze translates as "divine wind." The tactic was named after a legendary wind that protected Japan by sweeping away enemy invaders centuries earlier. In a kamikaze attack, a pilot intentionally flew into a target to cause major damage. The plane often carried bombs or extra fuel to create a bigger explosion.

A line of soldiers wades toward a waiting rescue ship at Dunkirk, France.

CHAPTER 4

The War on the Western Front

Hitler also wanted to expand westward. The German military swept across the Netherlands, Belgium, and France in May 1940. British forces at the Port of Dunkirk in France had to flee. Some Belgian and French troops went with them. The massive evacuation lasted from May 26 to June 4. More than 500,000 troops from Dunkirk and other ports were saved. By July, Germany controlled most of Western Europe, except for the island nation of Britain.

About 900 navy and civilian boats helped evacuate Dunkirk.

Battle of Britain

The fight over Britain began in June 1940 with bombings by the Luftwaffe. German planes first bombed British ports and ships, then airplane factories and the Royal Air Force (RAF). In September, the Luftwaffe started bombing London, Coventry, and other cities at night. These raids became known as the Blitz. RAF pilots defended Britain fiercely. In September, they were shooting down German bombers faster than Germany could build them. Defeated, Hitler called off the invasion in May 1941.

RAF fighter pilots came from all over the world, including Australia, Africa, and the Americas.

Landing craft bring supplies to troops on the beaches of Normandy, France.

D-Day

By 1944, Europe had been at war for more than four years. Germany controlled most of Western Europe, including France. Britain and its allies wanted to push back Germany, out of its captured territories. The Allies started by invading Normandy in France, across the English Channel from Britain. The massive invasion took place on June 6, 1944, which the Allies called D-Day. Nearly 200,000 troops landed along Normandy's beaches early in the morning.

Allied troops lead German soldiers who had been taken prisoner in Normandy, France.

Invasion of Normandy

D-Day was the first day in the Allies' massive invasion of Normandy. Both sides faced challenges during the invasion. Much of the Allies' supplies could not reach the beaches from the boats. Meanwhile, German forces were delayed because the Allies had attacked important bridges. This forced the Germans to take longer routes around the obstacles. There were also disagreements among German leaders, including Hitler and his top advisers. In the end, the Allies pushed through Normandy by the end of July.

Fooling Hitler

Hitler had long expected the Allies to invade France. However, he was not sure exactly where they would land. The Allies took advantage of this. They created a fake invasion, hoping to distract Hitler from the real one. The Allies made up troop movements to talk about on their radios. They even confused the German **radar** systems, making it appear as though ships were heading far north of the real troops that were sailing toward Normandy.

German troops move through a Belgian village during the Battle of the Bulge.

Battle of the Bulge

Allied forces moved from France across Belgium in August. They continued toward Germany's western border through the autumn of 1944. In December, the German army launched a surprise attack on Allied forces in France and Belgium. The battle became focused around the Ardennes mountains in southeastern Belgium. There, the Germans created a bulge as they pushed into a section of the Allied territory. This gave the battle its name, the Battle of the Bulge.

Days of cloudy skies made it difficult for Allied planes to attack or to gain information about German movements. However, Allied forces on the ground managed to halt German progress. The weather turned bitterly cold, and the German forces rapidly weakened. They finally gave in at the end of January. The battle resulted in around 80,000 American casualties, along with 1,400 British and more than 100,000 German casualties. Allied forces pushed into German territory, and the war was nearly over.

More people died in the Battle of the Bulge than in any other World War II battle.

American troops hide in foxholes, surrounded by snow, in Belgium.

The *Arizona* (pictured) and the *Oklahoma* warships were both destroyed in the Pearl Harbor attack.

CHAPTER 5

The War in the Pacific

In the Pacific, Japan planned attacks on territories in Asia and the South Pacific controlled by Europe and the United States. To keep the United States from fighting back, Japan attempted to cripple the U.S. Navy. On December 7, 1941, Japanese forces attacked the Pearl Harbor naval base in Hawaii. Japanese pilots sank two warships and damaged several others. Nearly 200 aircraft were destroyed. The United States declared war on Japan the next day.

The attack on Pearl Harbor lasted about two hours.

Midway

In June 1942, Japan planned additional attacks against Hawaii, British-controlled Fiji, and the Samoan Islands, which were controlled by the United States and New Zealand. Japan's navy would first ambush U.S. forces at Midway Island to clear the way. However, the U.S. Navy had broken Japan's code for secret communications and knew about the ambush. This gave U.S. forces a chance to prepare for the attack. They sank several Japanese ships. Japan lost nearly 250 aircraft and more than 3,000 troops.

Crew members of the USS *Yorktown* do repairs after an attack during the Battle of Midway.

Allied troops took about 1,000 Japanese soldiers prisoner at Guadalcanal.

Guadalcanal

By August, Japanese and American troops had become locked in a struggle on the island of Guadalcanal. The fighting lasted six months. During that time, there were seven naval battles and 10 land **campaigns**. The United States finally claimed victory in February when Japanese troops retreated off the island. The long fight harmed both sides. About 1,600 Americans were killed in the fighting. Japan lost 24,000 troops, as well as control of the Pacific war.

U.S. troops raised the American flag on Iwo Jima 31 days before the fighting was officially over.

Iwo Jima

By February 1945, Allied forces were planning the final air attack on Japan. First, the Allies needed to gain the tiny island of Iwo Jima, which was near Japan and controlled by it. From the island, Allied planes could take off very close to Japan. The Battle of Iwo Jima was fought on extremely rugged terrain. Japanese forces were protected with forts and miles of tunnels. The fighting lasted about a month before U.S. forces assumed control. The battle resulted in 6,800 American and nearly 20,000 Japanese deaths.

Okinawa

The last great battle in the Pacific took place on the island of Okinawa, south of Japan's mainland. The 82-day battle lasted from April through June 1945. Japan's defense against the Allies was desperate. Numerous Japanese airmen gave their lives in kamikaze attacks. Many Japanese troops and civilians decided to kill themselves rather than be captured. The fighting cost 12,000 American and more than 100,000 Japanese lives by the time U.S. forces claimed victory.

U.S. troops carry a wounded marine away from battle on Okinawa.

Exhausted marines drink cups of coffee after days of fighting at the Marshall Islands.

38

CHAPTER 6

Ending the World War

By 1945, war, disease, and famine had claimed nearly 60 million lives around the world. The Allied forces held advantages in Europe, North Africa, and the Pacific. However, the war was not over. The Allies planned a massive invasion of Japan. The events of the closing months of 1945 revealed the full horror of war.

About 70 million people in total fought for the Allies and Axis powers in World War II.

The Fall of Berlin

By 1945, German forces were retreating on two sides. To the east, they were retreating from Soviet forces. To the west, they were being pushed back by American, British, and other Allied forces. Germany's enemies were quickly nearing its capital of Berlin. By the end of January, Soviet forces were only 40 miles (64 kilometers) from Berlin. In April, British and American troops were 60 miles (97 km) from Berlin.

Timeline of World War II Battles

SEPTEMBER 1940
The Blitz begins in London and other cities in Britain.

JUNE 1941
German forces invade the Soviet Union.

DECEMBER 7, 1941
Japanese planes attack Pearl Harbor in Hawaii.

Allied forces surrounded Berlin on April 25. They moved into the city over the next few days. Inside the city, they met with little fighting. Hitler killed himself, and Germany's grand admiral of the navy, Karl Dönitz, was left in charge of the country. Dönitz quickly **surrendered**. The war in Europe was officially over on May 8, 1945. Today, the day is celebrated as V-E Day, or Victory in Europe Day.

JUNE 6, 1944
Allied forces land on beaches in Normandy, France, on D-Day.

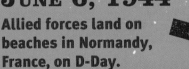

MAY 8, 1945
Germany surrenders.

AUGUST 6, 1945
U.S. forces bomb Hiroshima, Japan.

American planes drop bombs on Hakodate, Hokkaido, Japan.

Hiroshima and Nagasaki

Although the war in Europe had ended, the war in the Pacific continued. Starting in March 1945, the United States bombed Japanese cities at night. A raid on Tokyo alone killed nearly 100,000 people. Most of them were civilians. As the attacks continued, Japan became more determined not to give up. U.S. leaders planned an invasion of Japan's main islands for November 1945. They estimated, however, that tens of thousands of Americans could die trying to take over that country.

To avoid so many deaths, U.S. president Harry Truman decided to use a new weapon called the atomic bomb instead. On August 6, 1945, the United States dropped an atomic bomb on Hiroshima, Japan. The town of Nagasaki was bombed three days later. The destruction that these bombs caused was more than Japan could handle. Japan sent news on August 15 that they surrendered. World War II had finally come to an end. ★

The Soviet Union declared war on Japan two days after Hiroshima was bombed.

The atomic bomb wiped out about 90 percent of Hiroshima.

True Statistics

Lives lost in World War II: 60 million

Country that suffered the most casualties in the war: Soviet Union

Amount of bombs the Allies dropped between 1939 and 1945: 3.4 million tons

Number of people who served worldwide during World War II: 1.9 billion

Number of Americans killed in the Japanese attack on Pearl Harbor: About 2,400

Number of German casualties in the Battle of the Bulge: More than 100,000

Date of Victory in Europe (V-E) Day: May 8, 1945

Dates of Victory over Japan (V-J) Day: August 14 and August 15, 1945

Number of years World War II lasted: 6

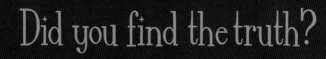

Did you find the truth?

T Germany lost more troops during the Battle of the Bulge than any other nation.

F All U.S. warships survived the attack at Pearl Harbor without damage.

Resources

Books

Demuth, Patricia. *What Was Pearl Harbor?* New York: Grosset & Dunlap, 2013.

Mayo, Jonathan. *D-Day: Minute by Minute*. New York: Atria Books/ Marble Arch Press, 2014.

Yep, Laurence. *Hiroshima: A Novella*. New York: Scholastic, 1995.

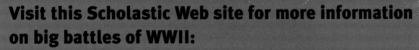

Important Words

campaigns (kam-PAYNZ) — organized actions in order to achieve a particular goal

casualties (KAZH-oo-uhl-teez) — people who are injured or killed in an accident, a natural disaster, or a war

civilians (suh-VIL-yuhnz) — people who are not members of the armed forces

dictator (DIK-tay-tur) — a ruler who has complete control of a country, often by force

evacuated (i-VAK-yoo-ate-id) — moved away from an area or building because it is dangerous there

expand (ik-SPAND) — become larger

infantry (IN-fuhn-tree) — the foot soldiers of an army

radar (RAY-dahr) — a way that ships and planes find solid objects by reflecting radio waves off them and by receiving the reflected waves

resources (REE-sors-iz) — things that are of value or use

siege (SEEJ) — the surrounding of a place, such as a castle or city, in order to cut off supplies and then wait for those inside to surrender

surrendered (suh-REN-durd) — gave up or stopped resisting someone or something

tactics (TAK-tiks) — plans or methods to win a game or battle or achieve a goal

Index

Page numbers in **bold** indicate illustrations

About the Author

Peter Benoit is the author of dozens of books for Children's Press. He has written about American history, ancient civilizations, ecosystems, and more. Peter is also a historical reenactor, occasional tutor, and poet. He is a graduate of Skidmore College, with a degree in mathematics. He lives in Greenwich, New York.